W9-DBI-200

CLASSIC ROCK T-SHIRTS

THIS IS A CARLTON BOOK

Text and design copyright © 2006
Carlton Books Limited

Material in this book has previously
appeared in *Vintage T-Shirts* (2006).

This abridged and updated edition
published in 2011
by Carlton Books Limited
20 Mortimer Street
London W1T 3JW

10 9 8 7 6 5 4 3 2 1

This book is sold subject to the
condition that it shall not, by way of
trade or otherwise, be lent, resold, hired
out or otherwise circulated without the
publisher's prior written consent in
any form of cover or binding other than
that in which it is published and without
a similar condition including this
condition being imposed upon the
subsequent publisher.

All rights reserved.

A CIP catalogue record for this book is
available from the British Library.

ISBN: 978 1 84732 919 6

Printed and bound in Dubai

Senior Executive Editor: Lisa Dyer
Managing Art Director: Lucy Coley
Copy Editor: Lara Maiklem
Production: Kate Pimm

CLASSIC ROCK T-SHIRTS

Over 400 vintage tees from the '70s and '80s

**LISA KIDNER
& SAM KNEE**

CANCEL

CARLTON

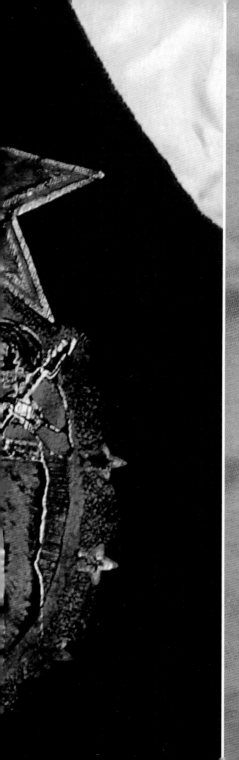

Contents

Foreword

'One Friday morning back in 2000, too early to mention, after setting up my 1980s 'girl' stall at Portobello Road in London, I met Sam over a pink 1980s Playgirl T-shirt he was selling on his American vintage clothing stall. He'd picked the shirt up on a recent buying trip to Texas, he gave me £5 discount and we've never looked back.'

Right Sam, me and the Playgirl shirt that started it all.

subject. Some purists may argue that certain acts are more rock than metal, more punk than new wave and so on. But ultimately this is a book of T-shirt design and not a lesson in rock history. The shirts are loosely grouped with the aim to capture a feeling in time and to suggest the mood of a youth scene.

We've closed our ears to the music, put personal taste aside and opened our eyes to create an objective overview of the 1970s and 1980s music scene. Although the popularity of the printed rock-and-roll band shirt exploded in the 1970s, the roots lie firmly in the 1960s. Mid 1960s 'invasion-style' groups like the Beatles dipped their toes in the T-shirt market, but it was the West Coast gig promoters, such as Bill Graham pushing local acts like the Grateful Dead, who first realized this emerging potential to sell T-shirts as well as gig tickets at venues.

For this book we dug deep – from Paris to New York, from Denmark to back home in London – to cream off the supreme shirts you see in this book. Our quest led us to design archives, dealers, true fans and hardcore collectors alike. For those of you who collect T-shirts, we discovered three types of collector in our research, and they seem to hold true across most genres of collecting, be it records, denim, trainers or books.

for a second wave.

Whatever the chosen method, we'd like to thank these fellow collectors, fans and brands for sharing their T-shirts with us. Without their help this task would not have been possible.

Take a close look at each T-shirt design for what it is – a piece of artwork – regardless of band association. You'll find everything from graphically purist post-punk shapes to fantastical metal fantasy art; from crude cut-and-paste art school designs, to full 1980s neon. Enjoy the crazy mix!

Lisa + Sam

feel the noize

Let it Rock

Above and right The Who tie-dye shirt, 1970, worn by Keith Moon on the cover of the album *Meaty Meaty Big and Bouncy*, 1971.

Rock is arguably the biggest thing to ever happen to the printed T-shirt. Born in the 1950s, rock fever spread like wildfire in the 1960s and by the '70s more records were being sold than ever before. The popular youth music of the day found mass appeal the world over. Rock merchandising became fashionable business, as it was all the rage to flaunt your taste in notes and chords on your chest. Rock is such a broad genre – from the progressive rock of Pink Floyd and the glam rock of Slade to the heavy rock of Led Zeppelin and the acid rock of the Grateful Dead – and we've tried to touch on all substyles beneath this vast umbrella. Rock forth and feast your eyes on a magic mix of classic rock tees.

Let there be light,
Sound,
Drums,
Guitar.
Let there be rock.

AC/DC, 'LET THERE BE ROCK'

Above Yardbirds, 1966. This shirt was originally owned by the late, great Greg Shaw and was worn at the Monterey festival in 1967.

Above The Who band logo shirt, 1974.

Above Mott the Hoople iron-on thermal-style T-shirt, 1972.

Above A Mercury Records promo shirt for Blue Ash, an underrated Ohio power-pop band, 1972.

Above Allman Brothers Band logo shirt, early 1970s.

Above Slade, Cum On Feel the Noize, silver glitter iron-on, 1973.

Above Free, London blues-rock group, early 1970s.

Above Led Zeppelin glitter iron-on band shirt, early 1970s.

Above Todd Rundgren, Go Ahead, Ignore Me, glitter screen-print shirt, early 1970s.

Overleaf, top row, left to right Bee Gees, Spirits Having Flown tour, 1979; Deep Purple, 1973/1974; Jackson Browne, 1974; Rolling Stones, USA tour, 1981. **Bottom row, left to right** Loggins and Messina, *Sitting In* album artwork T-shirt, 1971; Bruce Springsteen, *Darkness on the Edge of Town* period, 1978; the Beatles, *Sgt Pepper's Lonely Hearts Club Band* music film promo shirt, 1978; Emerson, Lake and Palmer, eponymous first-album artwork shirt, 1971.

SPIRITS HAVING FLOWN

BEE GEES

NORTH AMERICAN TOUR '79

DEEP PURPLE

LOGGINS MESSINA

BRUCE SPRINGSTEEN

The Dr Pepper Central Park Music Festival

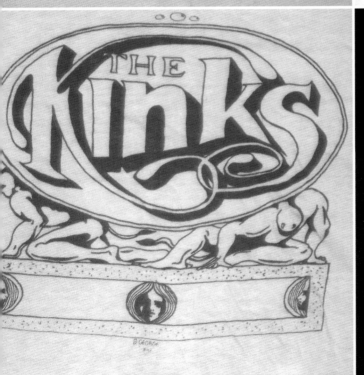

THE Kinks

The Schaefer Music Festival in Central Park

10TH ANNIVERSARY

Above Mick Jagger, All Right, iron-on pin-up shirt, 1976.

Above Mick Jagger iron-on shirt, early 1970s.

Above Mick Jagger iron-on print, 1979.

Above Pink Floyd, photographic glitter-edged iron-on, 1975.

Above and top Pink Floyd, Animals tour shirt, 1977.

Previous pages, top row, left to right Beach Boys, 1973; Elton John, 1973–1974; Slade logo, 1972; Dr Pepper Central Park Music Festival, 1978. **Bottom row, left to right** Led Zeppelin, 1973; Bee Gees, 1975; the Kinks, 1974; Schaefer Music Festival, 1975.

Above left and right Grateful Dead, spring concert at Amherst, Massachusetts, with Patti Smith Group and Roy Ayres Ubiquity, May 1979.

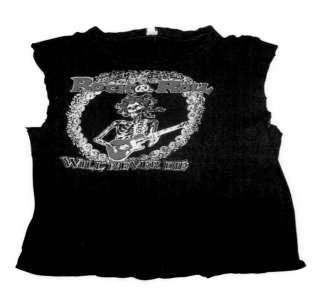

Above left and right Grateful Dead, Rock 'n Roll Will Never Die, Syracuse, New York tour, 1984.

Above and right Grateful Dead, European tour jersey shirt, 1981. The Dead were one of the first groups to set the trend for printing band T-shirts in the late 1960s.

Above left and right Grateful Dead, Jungle Weekend ringer shirt, 1978.

Above left and right The Beach Boys in Concert, 25th Anniversary tour shirt, 1985.

Above left and right The Eagles, Long Run tour shirt, late 1970s.

Above left and right A montage of classic Grateful Dead skull-based illustrations, 1979/1980.

Above left and right Tom Petty and the Heartbreakers, Live in Concert, cut-off jersey shirt, 1979.

Overleaf, top row, left to right Billy Joel, mid 1970s; ZZ Top, the 'Little 'Ole Band from Texas', early 1970s; Wings, Over America tour, 1976; Carole King, early 1970s.
Bottom row left to right Bee Gees, *Main Course* album-artwork promo shirt, 1975. Beatles, Let It Be NY festival shirt, 1970s; Dr Pepper Music Festival on the Pier, 1981; the Beatles, *Sgt Pepper's Lonely Hearts Club Band*, 1978.

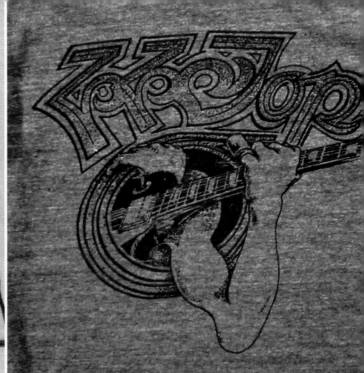

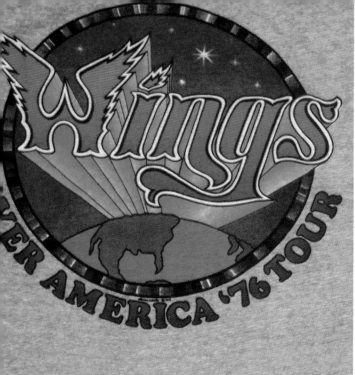

Wings
OVER AMERICA '76 TOUR

Carole King

Dr Pepper
Music Festival 1981
ON·THE·PIER

Sgt. Pepper's
LONELY HEARTS CLUB band

Above AC/DC, Bon Scott memorial iron-on, 1980.

Above Black Sabbath, 1970s.

Above Ozzy Osbourne, early 1980s.

Above Ozzy Osbourne, The Ultimate Sin, 1988 UK Tour.

Above Kiss, Crazy Nights 88, European Tour.

Above and top Kiss, Love Gun tour shirt, 1978. The *Love Gun* album artwork appears on the front of the shirt, while the back design is based on a famous press photo of the band, circa 1977.

Opposite Kiss, Rock 'n Roll Over tour shirt, 1976–1977. The tee was purchased at the band's historic first-time performing at Madison Square Garden, New York City, February 1977.

Above and top A very early unofficial Kiss shirt from 1977. Owned by Jon Rubin (see pages 32–33), it was probably won at a state fair carnival, rather than purchased at a Kiss concert. Note that the back of the shirt is printed in reverse, since the star painted on Paul Stanley's eye is on the wrong side – a common problem with the bootleg T-shirts.

COLLECTOR: Jon Rubin New York, USA
www.kissrocks.net

LK: Your Kiss collection is mindbending. When and how did you first get into Kiss music?

JR: Funny you should ask that, being that I can't remember a time when I *wasn't* into Kiss! It really stems back to my older brother literally taping pictures of all the members of the band onto my baby crib, probably sometime in 1975. A few years later, when Kiss was at their peak in the US, I could hear their music playing from my brother's room constantly and I loved the excitement and energy it possessed. I have distinct memories of sneaking into his room at the tender age of four and just staring at the colourful *Rock 'n Roll Over* and *Love Gun* album covers, which visually captured what the band was all about. My parents bought me the Kiss toy guitar in 1977 and it wasn't long before I was playing jumping around with it on tables and couches at any and all family functions, singing and air-guitaring to my favourite Kiss tunes. Just a year or two later, I was dragging my folks to the local record store to buy the new Kiss album for me. Between their fun, exciting music and intense comic book/horror imagery, you could say I was intrigued. Looking back on it now, almost 30 years later, I still understand exactly what it was that got me hooked at such a young age.

LK: What makes collecting Kiss so special?

JR: Kiss is truly one of the few bands who make collecting fun. They had four individual members who each had their own fans (partially modelled after the Beatles), so you have to realize that with Kiss everything is multiplied four times because everything came as a set of four. Sure, that's four times the money to spend, but also four times the coolness factor – a genius plan for sure! And their T-shirts were particularly striking because, just like their album covers and posters, they always featured the band members on the front accompanied by the prominent Kiss logo, always in bright colours and mesmerizing presentation. Because they were so marketable, it's no surprise that they were (and still are) one of the most merchandised bands in the history of music. Years after the original line-up has come and gone (twice now), the likenesses of the original four Kiss characters

Above A Kiss shirt from their Dynasty tour, 1979. Despite the shirt reading 'World Tour 1979' this shirt never made it off American soil due to the lukewarm response to the *Dynasty* album. The 1979 Dynasty tour marked drummer Peter Criss's last tour with the group and the end of the original line-up, not counting 1990's reunion. This shirt was available through the band's official fan club, the Kiss Army.

continues to be licensed and merchandised worldwide, which is a testament to the power of the branding they created. There are many other bands whose music and style I love and appreciate, but I would never think to collect anything of theirs, simply because there's no excitement to it.

LK: Do you collect any tees from other bands? Or are you a one-band guy?

JR: Kiss and only Kiss – I bought other shirts from other rock concerts I went to in the 1980s, and wore many of them at the time, but I never actually collected T-shirts of other groups simply because none of them had Ace, Gene, Peter or Paul on them!

LK: Do you remember your first Kiss concert or T-shirt?

JR: Absolutely. They're one and the same, March 9, 1984 at Radio City Music Hall in New York City. It was Kiss's big homecoming gig for the Lick It Up tour after taking off their make-up and, fittingly enough, my older brother (who got me into the band in the first place) surprised me with tickets and took me to the show. It was there that I bought my first Kiss T-shirt – a 1983–84 double-sided black tour tee, which was the ultimate souvenir of such a memorable and important night. Although we had terrible seats, I had the time of my life because I had been waiting to see them live for many years – and I have this concert T-shirt to prove I was there.

LK: What's on your 'wants' list? Is there a T-shirt out there you've never managed to get your hands on?
JR: There are many cool Kiss shirts from the 1970s that are hard to find and would probably be very expensive if located. I'm always keeping my eyes out for the super rare set of shirts offered from the 1978 solo album order forms (a simple single-sided black shirt with each member's face on the front – just $5 back then!). Also anything from the 1980 Unmasked tour, since the majority of that tour was overseas and featured the new drummer Eric Carr – two reasons that would make those shirts more collectible. I'd also really like any Kiss jersey with the three-quarter sleeves, a style/trend specific to only a few of their tours in the early to mid 1980s and therefore increasingly hard to find.

LK: Do you ever wear your shirts or do you store them away in a special place?
JR: I never wear any of the shirts, mostly because they would never fit these days! But truthfully, some of them feel so fragile that I hesitate to even handle them, let alone wear them. I don't see how the value could ever be preserved by wearing them. As for the caring of them, I don't store them in any special way; I just fold them neatly and keep them in a pile with the rest of my Kiss collection. And yes, the entire collection is located in my 'Kiss Room'!

LK: Do you buy tees both mint and love-worn?
JR: Mint condition for any collectible – especially a shirt – is always ideal, but ironically enough, with T-shirts half their character is how they were worn and clearly loved back in the day. Still, the overall quality and level of usage would affect the price of the item dramatically, which could affect my decision to purchase. If it's a really rare shirt in pretty rough condition, I would have to pass, but if it's in great shape overall and worn only a bit, it's probably a shirt I would like to have.

LK: Do you keep your collection to a specific period?
JR: Well, Kiss's golden years from 1976 to 1979 saw the first big boom of their merchandise, more specifically in 1978 when Kiss was the biggest band in America. The original line-up at this time, and the glory period associated with it, is what makes this 'make-up era' of Kiss merchandise worth the most, therefore the most collectible and desirable. The less popular 1980 to 1983 period, which featured a few different line-ups, may be considered less valuable because the band's peak had passed, but some of the merchandise from that period is worth more than something from 1977, only because it was not as mass produced and also in many cases available only overseas, specifically in Australia, from 1980 to 1981. Kiss's second make-up wave, beginning with the record-breaking 1996–1997 Alive/Worldwide Reunion tour, also yielded another round of major merchandising that a lot of people have grown fond of, probably because it reminded them of a time 20 years earlier when Kiss items were everywhere.

Above A shirt from the Kiss Asylum tour, 1985–1986.

LK: Do any of your tees have stories attached to them?

JR: Well, the 1976 to 1977 Rock 'n Roll Over tour shirt I have is one of my favourite – and possibly most rare – ones. It was purchased by my brother at Kiss's first time playing at New York's famous Madison Square Garden, 18 February 1977 [see pages 30–1]. Although I was too young to go to the show – and believe me I wanted to – it was only a few years later that I got the coolest hand-me-down yet. This is truly a vintage shirt from a very famous gig in Kiss's illustrious history.

LK: Which tee is the jewel in your crown?

JR: The 1982 to 1983 Creatures of the Night jersey is probably the most rare shirt I have, because it comes from a tour that was short-lived and also the only one to feature new members Eric Carr and Vinnie Vincent in full make-up and costume. Many major markets were skipped over for this tour, so shirts like this one were sold in much smaller quantities than your average Kiss tour shirt. I also would imagine that the Rock 'n Roll Over shirt I have (the one I inherited from my brother) is quite valuable, not only because of how old it is, but also because of the history of the actual gig and venue where it was purchased.

LK: What do you think about high-end vintage stores that inflate prices of 'fashionable' rock shirts?

JR: I think high-end vintage stores who find old concert tees and sell them for ridiculous prices are only making this market more collectible, in addition to somehow spreading the idea that these could be considered fashionable. If it gives more attention to older bands or somehow breathes new life into a name or logo, then that's pretty cool. But what does bother me about this trend is when an 18-year-old hottie is walking around in a Mötley Crüe T-shirt from 1984, but has no idea who's in the band or what songs they sing… not to mention the fact that she wasn't even born when this shirt was made. Something about that is not very genuine to me – but if she looks awesome in it (chances are good on that), then I could reconsider my position!

Above and top Kiss in Concert, Alive in '79 tour shirt.

Left and far left Cheap Trick, Midwest power-pop legends, tour shirt, 1981.

Below Cheap Trick, *In Color* LP advertisement, *Bomp* magazine, November 1977.

Opposite Cheap Trick tour shirt, 1980.

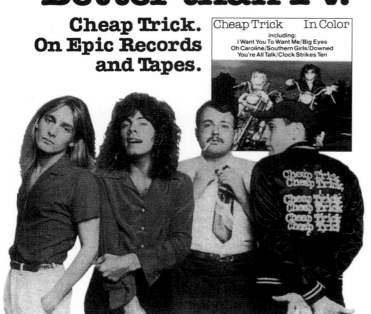

®"EPIC," MARCA REG. © 1977 CBS INC.

"Cheap Trick In Color." Better than TV.

Cheap Trick. On Epic Records and Tapes.

Cheap Trick — In Color
including:
I Want You To Want Me/Big Eyes
Oh Caroline/Southern Girls/Downed
You're All Talk/Clock Strikes Ten

"…(they) play rock like Vince Lombardi coached football…"
— **Rolling Stone**

"…hard as nails rock…not taken from stories in the Saturday Evening Post."
— **Hollywood Press**

"…destined for something great."
— **Trouser Press**

"…I play for everyone."
— **Rick Nielsen**

To see Cheap Trick for the first time is to be puzzled. To watch them perform is to be impressed. To know their new album is to join the ever-expanding universe of Cheap Trick fanatics.

"Cheap Trick In Color" is what made rock great in the first place: talent, hard work, inspiration and intensity. Robin, Tom, Bun E. and Rick each exemplify all of these qualities. Together, they have created a new music.

Produced by Tom Werman.

Above and top Cheap Trick, USA tour shirt, 1979.

Above Cheap Trick in Concert, 1980.

Above left and right Van Halen T-shirt, early 1980s.

Above left and right Meat Loaf, Bat Out of Hell concert shirt, 1978.

Above ZZ Top, She's Got Legs iron-on shirt, 1984.

Above ZZ Top, She's Got Legs band shirt, 1984.

Above and right ZZ Top Eliminator tour jersey shirt, complete with sleeve print, 1984.

GUNS N' ROSES

Above left and right Mötley Crüe, Girls, Girls, Girls, 1987.

Opposite Guns 'n Roses shirt featuring artwork for their first LP *Appetite for Destruction*, 1987.

Above Def Leppard and the Women of Doom, *Hysteria*-era band shirt, 1987.

Above left and right The Rolling Stones, promo shirt for the *Love You Live* album release, 1977.

Above left and right The Rolling Stones, She's So Cold and I'm So Hot shirts, depicting the ever-evolving classic tongue logo.

Above left and right Bon Jovi, 'You Give Love a Bad Name' promo shirt, 1986.

Above left and right Rod Stewart, Blondes Have More Fun shirt, advertising a three-night showcase concert in New York's Madison Square Garden, June 1979.

Above left and right Billy Joel, Live in NY, the Ameri-Canada tour, 1980.

Above and right Bruce Springsteen and the E Street Band, Born in the USA jersey tour shirt, 1984 –1985.

Live Aid 13 July, 1985

In July 1985, as a result of Live Aid, Run the World and Feed the World, more basic white T-shirts were sold in the UK than any year previously. In fact, so many shirts were sold to the supporting public that for the rest of the summer wholesalers were left exhausted and couldn't catch up with the demand.

Above left and right Live Aid, The Global Jukebox – This T-Shirt Saves Lives, 1985.

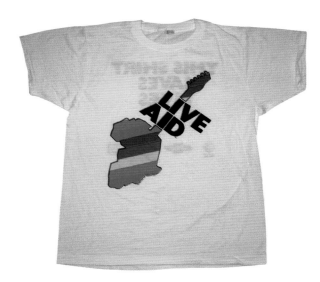

Opposite Crowd shot of Live Aid, Wembley Stadium, London, 1985.

Above left and right Live Aid, This Shirt Saves Lives, 1985.

Queen T-shirts

Above Queen World tour '76, featuring the famous Queen Crest band logo (based on Freddie Mercury's original design), and as seen on the *A Night at the Opera* album cover. This shirt emerged during the Japan and Australia tours of 1976.

Above Queen's USA tour, 1978. This shirt from the October–December tour of 1978 features the *Jazz* album artwork – that which spawned the infamous aforementioned nude bicycle race around Wimbledon Stadium.

Above Queen world tour 1978. Queen caused uproar in 1978 with their *Bicycle Race* video and 'Fat Bottomed Girls' song. This shirt, a souvenir from the huge tour, derives from that notorious and unforgettable footage.

Above Queen's USA tour 1976 for *A Night at the Opera*. The Crest logo has inspired countless Queen merchandise items over the years. This rare shirt originates from the USA tour that kicked off in January 1976.

Above Queen tour '75 shirt, featuring the very first Crest logo. This long-forgotten souvenir emerged in 1975 and is thought to be the only surviving example – but Brian's not selling it!

Above Queen spring tour '78 shirt. Simple, but no less striking, this *News of the World* album artwork-themed shirt originates from the European tour of 1978. The robot is a much-loved and iconic image.

Above Again a simple image, but a great example of one of the earliest known Queen T-shirts. This promotional item was issued by Elektra Records (in the USA) in 1974, and borrows from the artwork of the band's 1973 debut album.

Above Commemorating Queen's massively successful Works tour of 1984, this shirt features imagery from Fritz Lang's silent classic *Metropolis* – the film featured in Queen's *Radio Ga Ga* video of the same year. Yet another mega-rare item!

Above left and right Status Quo and Special Guests Live. The 1986 Magic Tour of Europe was one of Queen's biggest and most successful, and, alas, their last. Status Quo were the support for a number of the UK concerts. The entire tour sold out within hours.

Above left and right Featuring *A Kind of Magic* album artwork, this shirt, like most of the examples shown here, is much sought-after by collectors. The chances of finding one are negligible.

All T-shirts courtesy of the Brian May Archive, with special thanks to Greg Brooks and Richard Gray.

'80s Metal

Emerging from 1970s heavy rock bands, such as Black Sabbath and Deep Purple, 1980s metal brought a new electrically charged sound to a generation. Drums were loud, lyrics dark, the guitar was heavy and the beat was hard. This high energy resonated with a huge tribe of predominantly male youth searching for a more aggressive, fantastical form of escapism from the everyday grind. Lengthy, indulgent guitar solos were pivotal, as were horror-flick lyrics that took listeners from heaven to hell. The metal crowd had long hair, skinny jeans, high-top trainers, and their band T-shirts were worn tight. Here's a look at the metal mania shirts of the period.

Black is the night, metal we fight
Power amps set to explode
Energy screams, magic and dreams
Satan records the first note.
We chime the bell, chaos and hell
Metal for maniacs pure.

VENOM, 'BLACK METAL'

Opposite An absurd heavy-metal collage T-shirt of popular metal and rock acts of the day, late 1980s.

Above and top Venom, UK black metal band, USA Invasion tour shirt, 1984.

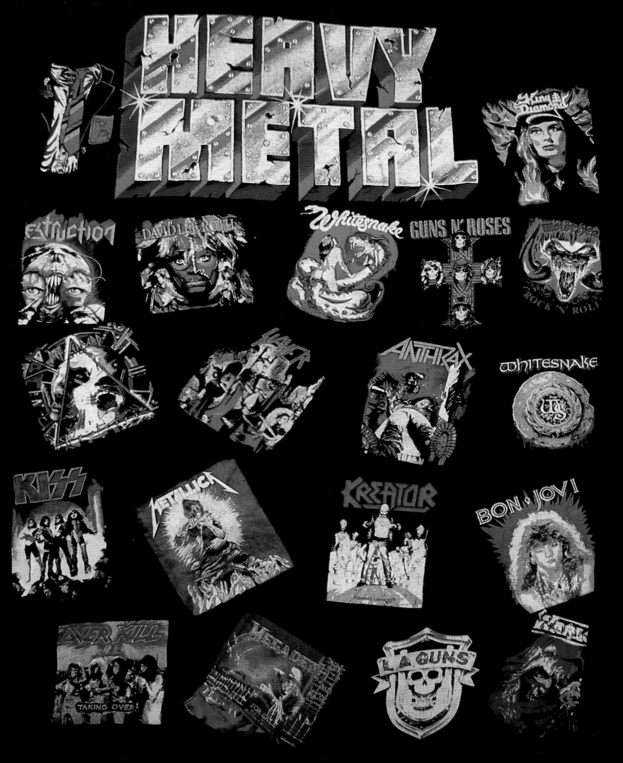

Above left and right Slayer, Hell Awaits tour shirt, 1985.

Above left and right Slayer, Slatanic Wehrmacht shirt, 1985. The Nazi connection made this shirt a little controversial, but it was also the name of their fan club.

Above Young Metal Attack shirt, the first-ever Metallica T-shirt, which was mainly given to band members and friends, early 1980s.

Above Iron Maiden: Monsters of Rock, 1988 World Tour.
USA, Canada, UK, Germany, Hungry, Austria, Holland, Switzerland, Italy, Greece, Spain, Portugal,
France, Denmark, Sweden, Finland, Norway, Australia, New Zealand, Japan.

Above Bon Jovi: Monsters of Rock
With DIO, Metallica, W.A.S.P., Anthrax and
Cinderella, 1987.

Above Iron Maiden, 1986.

Above Iron Maiden, The Number of the Beast, 1982.

Above left and right Metallica, European tour shirt for *…And Justice for All* album, 1988.

Above left and right Metallica, Ride the Lightening world tour shirt, 1984.

Above left and right Metallica, Damage Inc. tour for *Master of Puppets* album, 1986.

Above left and right Metallica, Metal Up Your Ass, 1985. The first-ever version of this shirt, bought at Metallica's debut performance at the Donington Monsters of Rock Festival in the UK.

COLLECTOR: Steve Gill, Stamford, England, www.Metallicaworld.co.uk

LK: What attracted you to metal?
SG: A friend of mine passed me a tape at school; it was a metal compilation. I fell in love with it straight away and I got this funny feeling when I heard it – it clicked. Before that I hadn't completely identified with any music specifically. I loved the aggression of it. It was loud, hard and heavy, different and full of energy. It was plugged into the mains. I wanted to find out more and I started collecting vinyl, then shirts.

LK: Your T-shirt collection is top-drawer. Do you wear the tees?
SG: To gigs, I mainly wear tees from the mid 1980s – the fit's right for metal look. The shirts were skinny in the 1980s, tight fit with cap sleeves. I sometimes wear these tees to gigs until they're wrecked, they fall to pieces, then I sew them back together and start again. The shirts got baggier in the 1990s and the shape changed. I still buy them, but they don't have the same skin-tight, metal shape.

LK: Do you buy 'boots' or official only?
SG: I buy official only, no bootlegs. I'll buy bootleg records, but never shirts. I don't collect any modern shirts either – modern meaning the last five years. I buy shirts from every show I go to, but I buy them just to wear, not to collect. When something's five years old, it becomes part of the collection.

LK: What's your best-ever score?
SG: The Young Metal attack shirt, definitely. It's the first Metallica logo T-shirt ever. I swapped for it – I had five or six great shirts from the Master of Puppets era, they didn't mean that much to me and a guy I knew was desperate for them. He had a friend who'd known the band from the beginning and he had the first ever Metallica shirt, so we traded. I just had to have it, and when I got it, I loved it.

LK: Are there any tees you could never part with?
SG: I've got a great old Ride the Lightening T-shirt that was owned by Scott Ian from Anthrax, so it's like the ultimate metal shirt. And there's a black Doris Pushead T-shirt from 1988 to 1989 that I wore to every show I went to from 1996 to 2004. There's something about that shirt that's full of attitude. I couldn't part with it as the memories from those shows are with the shirt.

LK: Was there a metal shirt you had to really dig around for, that was difficult to get your hands on?
SG: There's a Justice for All white shirt, 1988 to 1989 that Lars, the drummer, wore in a video on Metallica. I couldn't find it for ages. I had to really hunt around, and then two came up at once, so I got them both. I can wreck one, then start on the next.

Above and top Twisted Sister, Stay Hungry tour shirt, 1984/1985.

Above left and right Slayer, Live Undead, Dead Ahead tour shirt, 1985. This classic Slayer shirt design features the *Live Undead* EP cover artwork on the front and the tour dates for a short West Coast tour on the back.

Above left and right Slayer, Haunting the Chapel, 1986.

Redman Productions Presents

DIRTY ROTTEN IMBECILES

D.C.'s
BLACK MARKET BABY

RHYTHM PIGS

Appearing at:
THE COMPLEX

friday jüne 6

UNDERGROUND SCREEN PRINTS

Hardcore punk, thrash & crossover

Opposite Dirty Rotten Imbeciles gig shirt for the Complex venue. This shirt was made for just one show – the Complex in Washington DC, USA, in the summer of 1986.

Above Suicidal Tendencies skate-punk shirt, 1983.

Above Napalm Death, one of the first shirts made for the band, 1986/1987.

Above Cro-Mags, *Age of Quarrel* shirt, 1986. Not the first Cro-Mags shirt, but the first shirt that came out on release of the album.

Above Jody Foster's Army, Californian skate-punk tour shirt, 1985.

Above Black Flag, *In My Head* band shirt, 1985

Above left and right Black Flag, *Loose Nut* band shirt, 1985.

Opposite and above Monsters of Rock Metal Madness, a one-day UK festival featuring an all-star line-up, including Metallica, Van Halen and Scorpions, 1988.

Above Crumbsuckers, NY hardcore band, T-shirt artwork by Sean Taggart, late 1980s.

Above Accused, Panic in the Casket tour shirt, late 1980s.

Above left and right Anthrax, classic NOT-man skating design, *Among the Living* era, 1986/1987.

Above left and right Metallica white Doris shirt, designed by Pushead in 1988. This example has been cut down into a vest, but it is believed that the white shirt was released before the black one; they are very hard to find.

Above left and right Accused, Martha Sucks Brains shirt, late 1980s.

JERSEY SHIRTS

Well known in the USA, jersey shirts are baseball-style tees with three-quarter-length sleeves. They are most commonly tour shirts and were produced in abundance in the 1970s and 1980s. Nearly always double sided and sometimes even featuring extra sleeve prints, they are probably the most elaborate and decorated of all band shirts. Although mass produced at the time, they now have a cult following among T-shirt collectors. The style was used across all genres of music, from Motörhead to Michael Jackson, though they were particularly favoured by the stadium rock and metal bands of the era.

Above Black Sabbath, a *Sabbath Bloody Sabbath*-esque bootleg shirt. Back in the 1980s there was a slew of bootleg shirts available outside shows or at flea markets, county fairs, and so on. This is one from that era, but with a unique, noteworthy design.

Right and top Venom USA tour jersey, 1986, commemorating their 'seven dates of hell' for the *Possessed* album.

Above left and right Kiss jersey-style tour shirt, celebrating and promoting their 10th Anniversary tour, 1983.

Above left and right Judas Priest, Point of Entry tour jersey, 1981. It was on this tour that Iron Maiden opened for them.

Above left and right Judas Priest, Screaming for Vengeance tour shirt, 1983.

Above left and right Kiss band shirt 1979/1980. The front depicts Kiss in full make-up, while the back view shows rare unmasked illustrations. The sleeves have classic Kiss Army logo prints.

Above left and right Black Lace, lesser-known NY girl rock group, tour shirt for the *Unlaced* album, 1984/1985.

Above and right The Rolling Stones, jersey-style USA tour shirt,1981.

Above left and right Joan Jett, jersey shirt for her *Bad Reputation* album, 1981. Probably not official.

Above and right Megadeth, Peace Sells… But Who's Buying? tour jersey, 1986. Omid (see pages 88–91) bought this when Megadeth were touring with Dark Angel. 'When I wore this to school the next day (I was in eighth grade), the administration made me turn it inside out because of the back. "Rattle Your God Damn Head" was too much for them, I guess!'

Above and right Grim Reaper, Hell on Wheels tour shirt, 1987. Grim Reaper were part of a new wave of British heavy metal acts.

Above and right Slayer, Reign in Blood
shirt from their USA tour, 1986/1987.

Above left and right Metallica Doris character,
designed by Pushead, 1988.

Above and top Judas Priest, Defenders of the Faith tour jersey, 1984. This is a specially made, one-off shirt for the Washington, DC, shows, featuring great graphics of the White House and member Rob Halford on the Lincoln Memorial.

Above and right AC/DC, Fly on the Wall tour jersey shirt, 1985. The date of the gig the owner saw is highlighted in black marker on the back of the shirt.

Above and right Led Zeppelin, jersey-style band shirt, late 1970s.

Above Riot, Restless Breed tour jersey shirt, 1982. Riot was a classic New York-area hard rock/metal band.

Above and opposite Accept, Metal Heart tour jersey, 1985, bought when Accept were opening for Iron Maiden on the spring leg of their Powerslave tour.

Above and right Dokken, Rockin' America tour jersey shirt, 1987. This shirt came from the show where Dokken were opening for Twisted Sister, who were on their Come Out and Play tour.

LK: When did you first get into metal and rock music? Why did it strike a chord with you?

O: I first got into rock music when I was barely out of diapers, if I even was out of diapers! My mom is a big music head and I always credit her with getting me started. I grew up in a house where there was always music playing. I started getting 45s (the Guess Who, Elton John, etc.) back when I was a toddler and had a little toy record player to play them on. My love for the harder rock and heavy metal came in about third or fourth grade when my family moved back to the USA [from Iran], I got right into it. I think I was about eight when I got my first Kiss album in 1982. It was *Creatures of the Night*. It probably would have happened earlier if we hadn't moved to Iran for most of the late 1970s. Coming straight from a country where we'd just witnessed a revolution and then a war start, no wonder I was drawn to metal! So I was probably eight years old and found KISS, then got into the rest from there. It was an avalanche that has never stopped.

LK: What's the first music-related tee you can remember buying or being given ? How old were you? Was it from a specific concert?

O: Well, the first shirt I got was probably a Kiss iron-on shirt that I remember having to trade my friend in elementary school for some comics or something when we were about nine. I still have it, it's tiny! But the first true concert shirt I got was from Kiss on the Animalize tour, 27 November 1984 at the Baltimore Civic Center when they played with Queensryche. My mom took me – it was three days before my 11th birthday. So yeah, it totally killed, and I bought a shirt at that show and I still have and wear it today. It's the one with the grey sleeves with rings on – it's sort of visible in the picture of my wall of shirts.

LK: Which is the most important tee in your collection, the one with the most personal relevance?

O: Well, the most precious and personal to me is probably my Metallica, Ride the Lightning shirt that I'm wearing in the photo [opposite]. The story goes like this… I was in sixth grade, it was

right after my 11th birthday and a girl in my grade had an older brother Ryan, who was a diehard metal head. I remember going to his house and he just had so many great records, posters, shirts, import, crazy stuff that was hard to get back then – you had to really work to find this stuff! So one Sunday, 13 January 1985, I get a call from him out of the blue saying, 'Hey man, there's this show in Maryland this afternoon and we have three tickets, but no ride there – if you can get us up there, you can have the extra ticket.' The show was Metal Massacre 1985 that featured WASP, Metallica and Armored Saint. I have no idea how I managed to get my parents to agree to it, but somehow my Mom drove us the 45 minutes up to the club and dropped us off for the show. It was a life-changing experience. We were so young and small that we couldn't see, so we climbed up and were literally standing inside the PA on the stage, just getting shredded by the volume. It was incredible! Metallica blew me away, but I must admit at the time I was so into WASP that I bought a WASP tour jersey instead of a Metallica shirt.

Ryan, however, bought the Metallica shirt and a couple years later I remember calling him and asking him if he still had it, and if he would sell it to me. I bought the shirt for like $5.

LK: Are you precious with your tees, keeping them wrapped up and in mint condition, or do you wear them day to day?

O: Some of them, like the Runaways ones, I don't wear… they're so delicate now it's not a good idea. The rest, well, I wear them all. I wore the Metallica one I've just talked about for a recent show our band played, which was on the 20th anniversary of the show the T-shirt came from. I am a collector, so I do my best to keep them in good shape, but with shirts I do like to actually wear and share them.

LK: What's your t-shirt want list? Are there any you want, but can't track down, or any you'd die for?

O: Oh, I don't know… there's a few Runaways shirts I don't have that I'd love to find, like the 1977 Japanese tour shirt that looks like Cherie's corset! And they did a red 1976 European tour shirt I've always wanted. But for the most part I'm pretty happy with what I have. I mean, if I see something I like I'll buy it if it's reasonably priced, but I don't really have a list of stuff I'm searching for anymore!

LK: Does it annoy you that 'fashion people' are wearing old rock shirts often without knowledge of the bands or an appreciation of the music, and the crazy prices that shirts can go for in vintage clothing stores in Manhattan?

O: Well, quite honestly, yes. It did bother me for a long time. Sometimes I will still ask some hipster muffin on the streets of NYC if he's really into RATT, but I know the answer is almost always gonna be something that pisses me off, so I have stopped asking. When metal ruled the planet, we bought shirts and wore them because we loved the bands and the music; it wasn't a fashion statement or ironic in anyway. I have never worn a band shirt for any reason other than because I like the band. I don't really feel the need to get too worked up about this stuff anymore, though. I've already seen it happen once back in the

1980s when the first round of posers came through. There's more important things to worry about. Still, it is kind of annoying … what can I say? As far as the prices, yeah, some of them are crazy, and it's definitely peaking right now. It's just a trend though, it will pass like all trends do, and then the true and the few will still be standing there with their faded concert tees on.

LK: Do you think rock/metal peaked in the mid 1980s? What do you think of current stuff? Do you wear modern shirts?

O: Yes, I think that music in general peaked between the mid to late 1960s through to the mid to late 1980s. I feel fortunate to have caught the '80s and always bummed I missed the '60s and '70s. As far as what's happening today, I couldn't care less about most of it. I wear some modern bands, mostly just local bands or friends who I dig and support like Bad Wizard, Villains, Deceased, that kind of stuff. And I wear Battletorn shirts because I like our band. Even though Beverly (our singer) says it's a no-no, I support my own scene – I mean, if I don't like our band enough to wear a shirt, I shouldn't be in the band!

Above left and right The Runaways Invade Germany T-shirt, 1978. This shirt is believed to have been sourced from someone who worked for the group, and it's probably one of the few authentic Runaways tour shirts.

LK: Do you buy up tees because you like the design, whether it fits you or not?

O: Oh yeah, I've bought shirts that are too big, if it's one of a kind and I want to just have it for the stash. But that's pretty rare. As I said, I usually like to be able to wear them. Luckily I'm still able to fit into most of my old shirts.

LK: Do any of your other shirts have stories attached to them?

O: Many of my shirts came from shows I was at, so they all have memories attached. And then there's ones people have given me, which are important, too. They remind me of events, different times, friends… they tell a story of my path.

LK: Your Runaways collection is second to none. What makes you so into them in particular?

O: The Runaways just quite simply rule! I have been asked this question so many times, by so many people, and it's still one I can't elaborate on too much. I like to keep the answer kind of simple. Either you get it or you don't, but I personally feel they were revolutionary and unique in what they did. They just kick ass, good punk/hardrock delivered by hot young ladies – it was a great package. They paved the way for so many other bands. As far as why I chose them to get so deeply into, again, it was just something I felt I wanted to do and I did it. I'm an extremist, and if I do something it's usually all the way. I collected the Runaways all the way. I've found so much stuff on this band, which amazes me since they were around for less than four years and only released four studio albums and one live one in that time.

LK: Any last words about T-shirts, music or your collection?

O: Thanks for doing this book, it will allow people to see shirts that they may never have seen otherwise. Shirts are an important part of music history, of the whole package and scene, so it's cool that they're being seen as such! And as far as collecting, just have fun with it and try and stay true. By that I mean follow your heart, and not the trends… in music, and in life!

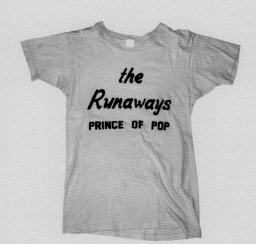

Left The Runaways, Prince of Pop T-shirt, 1975/76. Another iron-on letter shirt, this one was made for the famous scenester and DJ Rodney Bingenheimer who was a big part of the LA scene back at the time, and the subject of the film *Mayor of Sunset Strip* (2003).

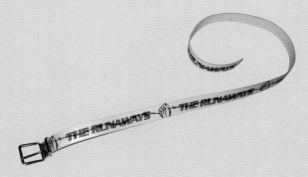

Above Original Runaways belt, *Waiting for the Night* promotional item, 1977.

Below And now… the Runaways. Sneakers promo item for the album of the same name.

Above right The Runaways Crawdaddy T-shirt, 1976. This was a custom-made shirt of the *Crawdaddy* magazine 1976 cover story on the band. There are many pictures of Joan wearing this shirt throughout the 1970s – she crossed out members as they quit.

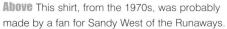

Above This shirt, from the 1970s, was probably made by a fan for Sandy West of the Runaways.

Above Not an official Runaways shirt, but one you could order from magazines. Note that Joan Jett is missing from the picture.

Above left and right The Runaways, Golden West Ballroom T-shirt. This shirt that was made by the venue, but has no specific date so it could have been from any of the shows between 1976 and 1978.

Above The Runaways, *Waiting for the Night* fan-made shirt, 1970s. This one belonged to Joan Jett and looks hand-drawn, but it's a silkscreen.

Above When the Runaways started in 1975, drummer Sandy West's mother made these shirts with iron-on letters. This was one of Joan's.

Above The Runaways, Atlanta shirt, 1978. A one-off, probably made by the venue or promoter – there were very few official tour shirts made.

Above Joan Jett's Golden West Ballroom shirt, 1976. As band members quit, she crossed them out or burned off their faces with cigarettes.

Above A sampling of Omid's Runaways memorabilia.

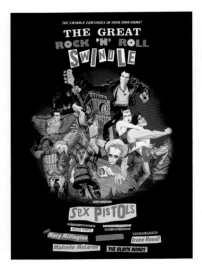

PUNK

In the mid 1970s punk arrived and breathed a breath of fresh air into the otherwise terminally dull decade that was still recovering from an excessive hangover of the excitement of the 1960s. At long last youth was on the rise again as the Pistols and their peers reflected the hopes, dreams, fears and personal politics of the generation. Not since the mid 1960s mod, beat group scene had British youth projected so much raw energy – the kids had temporarily lost their minds in a hippie-fuelled drug haze around 1968. The Sex Pistols, Clash and Ramones need little introduction, and their greatness cannot be denied.

Left *The Great Rock 'n Roll Swindle*, artwork of the posthumous Pistols cash-in flick, 1980.
Below The Sex Pistols line-up, 1977.

Above left and right I Survived shirt, from the Sex Pistol's first, and last, USA tour in 1978. It was most famously worn by drummer Paul Cook in the film *The Great Rock 'n Roll Swindle*.

Above and opposite Ramones shirt, bought on London's Kings Road in 1977.

Sons of Scuzz Hit Home
Run in World Punk Series

Opposite The Clash, 1977. An early shirt depicting their first LP cover artwork plus scenes from the Notting Hill riots in London the previous year.

Above PiL, Public Image Limited, 1979, ex-Pistols John Lydon's project.

Above Ramones band shirt, early 1980s.

Above Unofficial Ramones shirt, late 1970s. Ramones' shirts have been 'booted' to death.

new wave
& beyond

Punk rock was the spark for a genuine youth phenomenon. It seemed as if the world had changed almost overnight and that the movement had stirred the imaginations of the kids. As a result new bands, indie labels and magazines emerged from this new wave of inspired talent. This collection of shirts explores some of the resulting underground subgenres that divided, multiplied and followed well into the 1980s.

Above Kapatalist, 1977. A New York record label and home of early punk band Chain Gang.

Above Stiff Records label, 1977. This broad-minded indie label formed in July 1976, releasing early records by Devo, Ian Dury, Motörhead and Elvis Costello.

Above Max's Kansas City, 1976, the legendary NY music venue.

Above The Milkshakes, 1982.
This band from Chatham, Kent,
UK was formed by Billy Childish
in 1980 from the ashes of the
Pop Rivets.

Above The Milkshakes, 1981. The band created
a truly authentic, early '60s-sounding raw beat,
R&B sound and image.

Above Logo T-shirt from *BOMP!* magazine, 1977. Originally called *Who Put the BOMP!*, this 'zine was the brainchild of Greg Shaw and targeted true rock 'n roll fans. It was the first magazine to teach readers about 1960s garage punk records and to document the new wave of punk.

Right Original *BOMP!* T-shirt mail-order advertisement, featuring Steve Martin, 1977.

Above Lou Reed T-shirt, issue one artwork from *Punk* magazine, January 1976. The mag ran in the USA for 15 issues until June 1979.

Above *Sounds*, the now defunct weekly rock newspaper, T-shirt, 1983. It depicts a drawing by Savage Pencil of the youth styles of the day – punk, psychobilly, mod, and so on.

Above Sire records promo shirt, listing the labels' new wave signings, 1977.

Above Famous logo shirt from *Creem* magazine, mid 1970s.

Above ESG band shirt, 1981. This was a Bronx-based, sister no-wave quartet.

Above The Get shirt, DIY post-punk group, 1980.

Above San Francisco experimental art group, the Residents, Mark of the Mole shirt, 1981.

Above The Residents, Mole Show tour, October 1982.

Above Throbbing Gristle, early industrial noise, 1978.

Above The Residents, 1982. *Santa Dog* was released on their own label, Ralph Records.

Above The Residents, Coming in October, *Eskimo* album promo shirt, 1979.

Above The Modern Lovers, Jonathan Richmond's proto-punk outfit, mid 1970s.

Above The Damned, famous for releasing the first UK punk single, 'New Rose', drum logo shirt, 1977.

Above Ian Dury and the Blockheads, Blockhead logo shirt, 1978.

Above Chelsea, early London punk group headed by ex-porn star Gene October, band shirt, 1978.

Above The Dead Boys band shirt, 1977. A classic Ohio punk band formed from the ashes of Rocket from the Tombs and fronted by Stiv Bators.

Above Crime, early San Francisco punk band, 1976.

Above The Stranglers, *Feline* album artwork shirt, 1982.

Above The Stranglers' last Reading Rock shirt, 1983.

Above The Stranglers, *Aural Sculpture* album shirt, 1984.

Above Back shot of the Stranglers' Dramatise Tour shirt, 1988.

Above Joy Division, Manchester post-punk group, *Unknown Pleasures* album artwork shirt, 1979.

Above left and right Bauhaus, 'Bela Lugosi's Dead' 12-inch single promotional shirt from Small Wonder Records, 1979.

Above Factory Records logo T-shirt, early 1980s. Founded in Manchester, England, in 1978, signings included Joy Division and New Order.

Above New Order's *Movement* album shirt, 1981.

Above New Order's 'Procession' single artwork shirt, 1981.

Opposite and above Ciccone Youth,
Sonic Youth side project, 1986.

Above Sonic Youth, experimental rock/noise
group, Sister '87 tour shirt, 1987.

Above left and right Spacemen 3, For All the Fucked-Up Children of this World, 1989.

Above The Justified Ancients of MuMu, electronic sampling act that evolved into the KLF, 1988–1989.

Above E, Can You Feel It?, late 1980s drug-exploitation shirt.

Above Acid E, acid-house craze shirt, late 1980s.

superstars of the '70s

The early 1970s saw an emerging generation of young music fans looking for new celebrity personas that they could identify with – artists with a rebellious edge that could offer escapism and excitement to bored teenagers. The following acts offered exactly that. They were musical stylists and visionaries with a theatrical and artistic edge, hugely successful but never middle of the road.

Above left and right Iggy Pop, former Stooges lead man, *Lust for Life* album promo shirt, 1977.

Above Blondie iron-on shirt from 1978. Blondie was the pin-up girl of the 1970s and adorned the walls and T-shirts of countless teenagers.

Above David Bowie world tour shirt, 1978. This brief tour included music from both *Low* and *Heroes*.

Above Early to mid 1970s Bowie tee, probably a bootleg as the design bears little resemblance to officially released artwork.

Above David Bowie, *Station to Station*-era shirt, 1976.

Above left and right Lou Reed, Rock 'n Roll Animal, early 1970s. Solo shirt from the former Velvet Underground frontman.

Above Blondie, Blondie is a Group, from the power-pop *Parallel Lines* period, 1978.

Above Blondie, Live in Concert full-colour, iron-on T-shirt, 1980. Probably from the *Autoamerican* period.

Above David Bowie, 1983. Peculiar print depicting Bowie's changing image, including Ziggy glam rock as well as the *Let's Dance* era.

Above Bowie photographic iron-on, probably from the *Heroes* or *Lodger* periods, late 1970s.

Above Bryan Ferry, early solo shirt, mid 1970s.

Above Blondie, shirt from the 'Eat to the Beat' period, 1979.

Above left and right David Bowie, Glass Spider European tour shirt, 1987.

Above left and right David Bowie, Serious Moonlight tour shirt, 1983. This was the tour of the hugely successful *Let's Dance* album.

Above left and right Roxy Music, European tour shirt for their final album, *Avalon*, before the band dissolved, 1982.

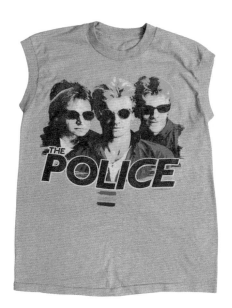

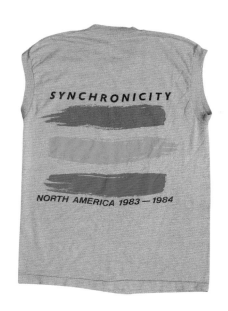

Above left and right The Police, Synchronicity North American tour, 1983–1984.

Above Bryan Ferry, *Boys and Girls* solo album shirt, 1985.

Above Bryan Ferry pin-up shirt, early 1980s.

Above left and right Bryan Ferry promo shirt for the *Solo* and *Roxy* compilation, 1988.

Above Bryan Ferry illustrated print tee, from early 1980s.

Above Roxy Music, *For Your Pleasure* album artwork shirt, late 1970s.

Above and top Blondie, Tracks Across America jersey tour shirt for the *Hunter* album, 1982.

New Romance

A uniquely British scene, the New Romantics emerged in the UK as a reaction to the grim reality of the second wave of UK punk. A pretty broad term as well as a 'movement', New Romantics can be used to conjure up the period of cultural change as the 1980s dawned. It combined the glamour of early 1970s Ziggy-style Bowie with Kraftwork-esque futuristic, synthesized sounds – the guitar became a secondary instrument as the synthesizer and electronics took centre stage. This overtly flamboyant scene saw groups emerge from London club life to high budget, opulent videos and major chart success.

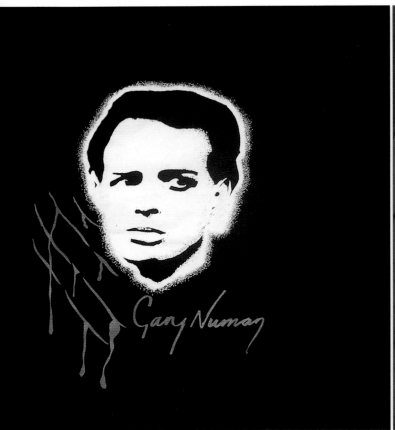

Above Gary Numan, UK electro pop pioneer, from the *Pleasure Principle* era, 1979.

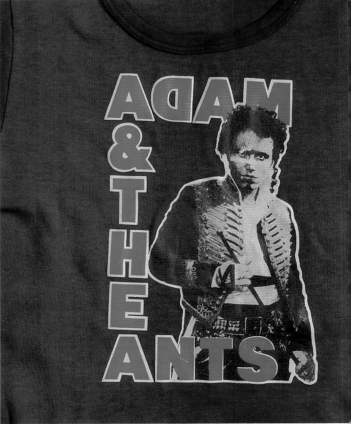

Above Adam and the Ants, *Kings of the Wild Frontier*, 1980. The Ants evolved from art-school punk into New Romantic chart-toppers at the start of the '80s

Above Adam Ant, shirt from the *Stand and Deliver* period, 1981.

Overleaf, top row, left to right Teardrop Explodes, Liverpool-based 1980s psychedelic-tinged group fronted by Julian Cope, 1981–1982; Nina Hagen, off-the-wall German artist who created a dissonant mix of punk, funk and opera, 1982–1983; Frankie Goes to Hollywood, Only Frankie Can Stop Me Now, 1984; Soft Cell, synthesizer duo, 1981.
Bottom row, left to right Culture Club, from the *Colour by Numbers* era, 1983; Wham!, seen by many as the ultimate early 1980s pop group, Young Guns shirt, 1982; Ultravox, from the *Systems of Romance* era, 1978. Echo and the Bunnymen, iron-on shirt, early 1980s.

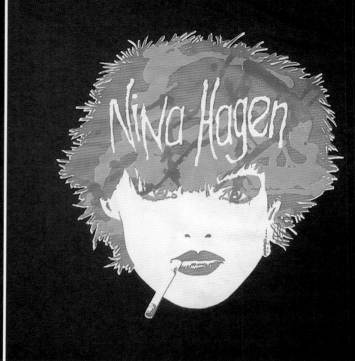

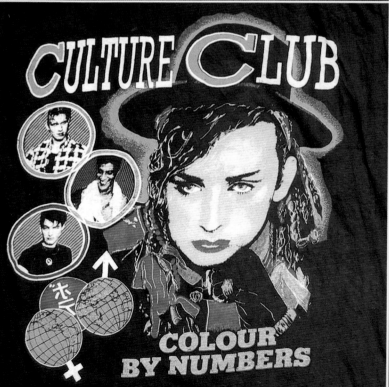

ONLY FRANKIE CAN STOP ME NOW!

FRANKIE GOES TO HOLLYWOOD

SOFT CELL

ULTRAVOX ULTRAVOX

ECHO AND THE BUNNYMEN

Above Bananarama, fun-filled 1980s pop girl group, early 1980s.

Above The Human League, the ultimate
1980s synth pop band, 1981.

Above Eurythmics, 1983.

Above Adam and the Ants, *Prince Charming* period, 1981.

Above Wham!, iron-on T-shirt, 1982–1983.

Above Illustrated iron-on of John Taylor, Duran Duran pin-up, early 1980s.

Above left and right Duran Duran, Coca-Cola-sponsored USA tour, featuring the band's first major stadium dates in America, 1984.

Above left and right Duran Duran, *Reflex* period USA tour shirt, 1984.

Above Duran Duran frontman Simon Le Bon in *Rio*-style graphics, 1982/1983.

'80S MEGASTARS

During the 1980s, three solo artists in particular made the rapid ascent to global superstar status. Madonna, Prince and Michael Jackson became more than musicians, solo artists or teen idols – they created a new level of megastardom, becoming extravagant style icons with an almost super-hero-like appeal. The launch of MTV in 1983 fuelled these years of image revolution and proved to be the perfect vehicle for transmitting their flamboyant characters directly into peoples homes, selling their music through groundbreaking cinematic-style videos.

Above left and right Michael Jackson, *Thriller* album promo shirt, 1982.

Opposite Young Michael Jackson fans wearing *Thriller* video-style gear, 1983.

Above Michael Jackson, *Thriller* T-shirt, 1982.

Above Michael Jackson, 'Billie Jean' video-style illustration, 1984.

Above Michael Jackson, *Thriller* full-photo iron-on, 1982.

Above Michael Jackson, sleeveless T-shirt, 1982.

Above and top Michael Jackson, unique 'Billie Jean' jersey shirt, 1983.

Above Prince, 'When Doves Cry' single promo shirt, 1984.

Above Prince, *Purple Rain* album T-shirt, 1984.

Above left and right Prince and the Revolution, 'Kiss' single from the *Parade* album, 1986.

Above Madonna, UK Live transfer shirt, 1987.

Above Madonna, *True Blue* album artwork shirt, 1986.

Above left and right Madonna, the Virgin tour, 1985.

Above left and right Madonna, the Virgin tour picture-disc print, 1985.

Above Madonna, world tour T-shirt, 1987. The *Who's That Girl* album was the soundtrack to the movie of the same name starring Madonna. Featuring four Madonna tracks, the album also included Club Nouveau and Scritti Politti.

Above Madonna, Who's That Girl world tour shirt, 1987.

Above Madonna, Who's That Girl world tour vest, 1987.

Above Madonna, Who's That Girl world tour shirt, 1987.

Above Madonna, Who's That Girl world tour shirt, 1987.

Above Madonna, early shirt from her first album, 1983.

Above Madonna, Strike a Pose illustration, late 1980s.

Above Madonna, early illustration transfer from the 'Lucky Star'/'Borderline' phase, 1983–1984.

Above Madonna, Italians Do It Better slogan shirt as worn in the *Papa Don't Preach* video, 1986.

Above Madonna, Who's That Girl world tour shirt, 1987.

Above Madonna, Who's That Girl world tour shirt, 1987.

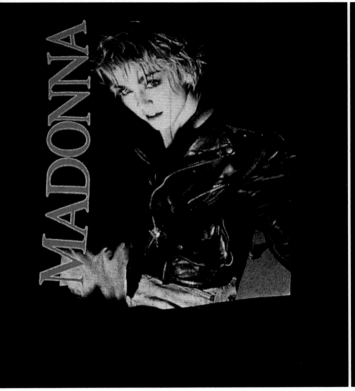

Above Madonna, 'Papa Don't Preach' shirt, 1986.

Above Madonna, 'La Isla Bonita' shirt, bought in 1987 from a show at Le Parc de Sceaux, France.

MADONNA COLLECTORS:

WAYNE STANDALOFT New York, USA

KELLY SMITH Virginia, USA

I've been to every Madonna tour since Who's That Girl at Wembley Stadium, London, in 1987 – I was 10 years old and it was my first concert ever! I was begging for tickets, but my parents said I was too young. Then, on 18 August, my Dad took me for a drive and we ended up in Wembley. He handed me two tickets; I was speechless. There were 80,000 people there that day and my Dad put me on his shoulders and got to the front of the standing area. I got most of the Who's That Girl T-shirts at the show; my favourite is the one with only her eyes.

I've been a Madonna fanatic since 1983. I first heard Madonna's single 'Holiday' in 1983 and thought, 'Who is that girl?' And recently I met her! I won a contest through Icon magazine; I got an invitation to the Bergdorf Goodman/UNICEF party that Madonna hosted. It was a dream come true. I have a picture that was taken of Madonna and me sitting there on the couch, chatting away. The whole thing was so surreal; it was like being Cinderella going to the ball. Madonna is breathtaking. My first words to Madonna were, 'I've been a fan of yours for 20 years.'

FRED GILLOTTEAU Paris, France

I started collecting in 1985. At the beginning I bought magazines and singles, but my first T-shirt was the 'La Isla Bonita' shirt. Madonna has incredible willpower, she wants to be the best, every time, and I like that. When the Re-Invention tour was in France, it was in Paris for four nights, from 1 to 5 September, 2004. The first night I actually had eye contact with her. Finally, at the end of the song 'Crazy for You', she threw her T-shirt in my direction and I caught it – it was fantastic, like a present for my 20 years of support.

Def Jam Recordings

Seminal record label Def Jam came about in 1984 and was founded by producer Rick Rubin and Russell Simmons. Label signings included Public Enemy, Run DMC and the Beastie Boys. The commercial explosion of this label in the mid to late 1980s brought hip hop to a much wider multicultural audience and into the realms of the mainstream. The slick logos from this time were the target of countless bootleggers in the boom years. No black item of clothing was safe, as the simple white logos were emblazoned across almost any garment available.

Above left and right Beastie Boys, *Licensed to Ill* album promo shirt, 1986.

Above left and right Enemy logo shirt, late 1980s. The seminal hip-hop group Public Enemy was formed in New York in 1982.

Above left and right Public Enemy, classic logo shirt, late 1980s.

Above left and right Public Enemy logo shirt, late 1980s. The instantly iconic logo was designed by Chuck D and depicts E Love (LL Cool J's sidekick) in the sights of a high-power rifle.

Above left and right Public Enemy band shot, all-over print tee, late 1980s.

Above Def Jam Recordings, record label logo shirt, 1986.

Above left and right Beastie Boys, Get Off My… band logo T-shirt, 1986.

Above Run DMC Adidas sponsorship shirt, 'My Adidas' *Raising Hell* period, 1986.

Above Beastie Boys, transfer-print shirt with newspaper clippings about their bad behaviour during their first UK tour, 1986/1987.

Above Beastie Boys T-shirt featuring artwork from their first LP gatefold, 1986.

Index

Figures in italics indicate captions.

Acknowledgements

T-shirts & Materials

We would like to thank the following sources for the loan of T-shirts and archive materials.

Aaron Fisher: 141
Aaron Lacey: 40T, 49B, 66
Aco: 12BL, 20B, 21, 23T, 120B
Brian May: 50–3
Camo Pete: 105TR, 110–1, 119BL, 124B
Cassie Mercantile: 22, 84B
Chris Charlesworth: 10
Colette Robertson: 128
Dean Engmann/shutemdown.com: 154–5
Duncan Watkins: 125T
François Dirty South: 55, 135BR
Frédéric Gilloutteau: 149R
Gary Smith: 100BL, 106TR, 108BR
George Castrinos: 24TR
Jon Rubin: 30–35, 78T
Kelly Smith: 145, 146BL, 148B, 149L
Lynn Berat, Dr: 91B, 14T, 14BL, 15TL, 15B, 16–7, 24TL, 24B, 25, 46B, 47T
Mandy Revill: 126
Nick Pankhurst: 41B
Nik Kukushkin at www.slayersaves. com: 56T, 67B
Omid: 13TL, 45T, 54, 56B, 67T, 68, 69B, 73B, 74, 75B, 75–6, 78B, 80T, 81–2, 83T, 84, 84T, 85–95
One of a Kind: 13BL, 118
Paul Burgess: 98–9, 101, 157
Paul's Place, Arch 53, Camden Market: 14TR, 23B, 36–39, 40B, 42, 47B, 79T, 80B, 112
Pete Wilkins: 114–5
Private collector NYC: 11T, 12T, 12BR, 13TR, 13BR, 19, 72, 73T, 102–4, 105TL, 105B, 106TL, 106B, 107, 108TL, 108BL, 109, 113, 116–7, 121, 142
Rob Pugh, Old School Vintage Boutique: 69T, 70–1
Seditionaries Ltd: 124T
Stephanie Barnett: 49T
Steve Gill: 57, 62–3, 75T, 83B
Vintage Vantage: 157T
Wayne Standaloft: 144, 146, 147T, 147BR, 148T

Bibliography & Text Credits

Thanks go to the following sources and publications for their extracts and contributions.

AC/DC, 'Let There Be Rock', 1977, Sony: 11
Kiss captions, courtesy Jon Rubin: 30–4
Queen introduction and captions, courtesy Brian May, with thanks to Greg Brooks and Richard Gray: 50–3
Runaways text, courtesy Omid: 88–95
Venom, 'Black Metal', 1982, Neat Records: 54

Picture Credits

We would like to thank the following sources for their kind permission to reproduce the pictures in this book. All other photographs © Carlton Books, with grateful thanks to Russell Porter.

Alexandra Giarraputo: 88
BOMP! magazine: 36B, 104.
Brian May archive/Richard Gray: 50–3
Chris Charlesworth, rear album sleeve from the Who's *Meaty Beaty Big and Bouncy*: 10
Corbis Images: Lynn Goldsmith: 138
Frédéric Gilloutteau: 150
Getty Images: Hulton Archive/Dave Hogan: 48
Jon Rubin: 30–35, 78T
Kelly Smith: 150
Lisa Carpenter: 30–34
Omid: 90–5
Private Collection: Courtesy of Shout! Factory/Sony BMG Music Entertainment: 96T
Private Collector, NYC: 11T, 12T, 12BR, 13TR, 13BR, 19, 72, 73T, 102–4, 105TL, 105B, 106TL, 106B, 107, 108TL, 108BL, 109, 113, 116–7, 121, 142
Redferns: Virginia Turbett: 96B
Steve Gill: 57, 62–4
Wayne Standaloft: 144, 146, 147T, 147BR, 148T

Every effort has been made to acknowledge correctly and contact the source and/or copyright holder of each picture and Carlton Books Limited apologizes for any unintentional errors or omissions, which will be corrected in future editions of the book.

Author Acknowledgements

Firstly we'd like to thank all collector nuts out there – keep the faith – in particular the hoarders who took the time to share their gems with us. François Dirty South, Jon Rubin, Steve Gill, and the 'madonnalicious' Kelly Smith, Fred and Wayne.

To Omid the Great: endless thanks for sharing his Monster collection and going the extra mile – keep on rockin'. Also thanks to Rob Pugh, Aaron, Chris Chalesworth, Dean Engman, Nik at slayersaves. com, Pete Wilkins, the anonymous private collector in NYC, Paul Burgess, Siobhan, Zoe, Teresa and Marcus, you're the stars, and Lynn for the shirts and that midnight call that saved us when technology failed.

Additional thanks to Brian May for sharing his rarely seen, rockin' collection of Queen tees and to Greg Brooks and Richard Gray for making it happen.

Where it all began, Notting Hill: thanks to Cassáie Mercantile and One of a Kind for loaning some of their rare treasures.

Calvin 'The Sacks' Holbrook, we know it was painful, but we couldn't have done it without you. Alice, the most beautiful girl in the world. Apologies to those we may have missed; don't take it personally.